JOYCE TYLDES

EGYPTIAN GAMES AND SPORTS

SHIRE EGYPTOLOGY

Cover illustrations
Top left: Middle Kingdom faience hippopotamus. (Cairo Museum)
Top right: Limestone *mehen* board and playing pieces. (British Museum)
Bottom: An Old Kingdom scene of fishermen jousting. (Cairo Museum)

British Library Cataloguing in Publication Data:
Tyldesley, Joyce A.
Egyptian games and sports. – (Shire Egyptology; 29)
1. Games – Egypt – History
2. Sports – Egypt –History
3. Egypt – Social life and customs – To 332 B.C.
I. Title
790'. 0932
ISBN-13: 978 0 7478 0661 5.

Published in 2007 by
SHIRE PUBLICATIONS LTD
Cromwell House, Church Street, Princes Risborough,
Buckinghamshire HP27 9AA, UK.

Series Editor: Angela Thomas.

Number 29 in the Shire Egyptology series.

ISBN 978 0 7478 0661 5.

First published 2007.

Printed in Malta by
Gutenberg Press Limited, Gudja Road, Tarxien PLA 19, Malta.

Contents

ACKNOWLEDGEMENTS

I would like to thank Mrs Angela Thomas and Dr Steven Snape for their unflagging help and support as I wrote this book. Dr Patricia Spencer of the Egypt Exploration Society cheerfully provided interesting information about ancient Egyptian dance. All uncredited photographs have been supplied by Rutherford Picture Library. The dynastic chronology is based on that of Dr William J. Murnane and acknowledgement is made to him and to Penguin Books for its use here.

List of illustrations

Chronology

Predynastic Period	*c.*5000-3300 BC		
		5000-4000	Badarian
		4000-3500	Naqada I
		3500-3300	Naqada II
Protodynastic Period	*c.*3300-3050 BC		
Early Dynastic Period	3050-2686 BC		
		3050-2890	First Dynasty *Narmer* *Aha* *Djer* *Den*
		2890-2686	Second Dynasty
Old Kingdom	2686-2181 BC		
		2686-2613	Third Dynasty
		2668-2649	*Djoser*
		2613-2498	Fourth Dynasty
		2613-2589	*Sneferu*
		2498-2345	Fifth Dynasty
		2345-2181	Sixth Dynasty
		2278-2184	*Pepi II*
First Intermediate Period	2181-2040 BC		
		2181-2040	Seventh to Tenth Dynasties
		2134-2060	Eleventh Dynasty (Theban)
Middle Kingdom	2040-1650BC		
		2060-1991	Eleventh Dynasty
		1991-1782	Twelfth Dynasty
		1897-1878	*Senwosret II*
		1782-1650	Thirteenth and Fourteenth Dynasties
Second Intermediate Period	1650-1570 BC		
		1650-1555	Fifteenth and Sixteenth Dynasties (Hyksos)
		1663-1570	Seventeenth Dynasty (Theban)

New Kingdom	1570-1070 BC		
		1570-1293	Eighteenth Dynasty
		1570-1546	*Ahmose*
		1524-1518	*Tuthmosis I*
		1504-1450	*Tuthmosis III*
		1498-1483	*Hatshepsut*
		1453-1419	*Amenhotep II*
		1419-1386	*Tuthmosis IV*
		1386-1349	*Amenhotep III*
		1350-1334	*Akhenaten*
		1334-1325	*Tutankhamun*
		1325-1321	*Ay*
		1293-1185	Nineteenth Dynasty
		1279-1212	*Ramesses II*
		1193-1187	*Siptah*
		1185-1070	Twentieth Dynasty
		1182-1151	*Ramesses III*
		1141-1135	*Ramesses VI*
		1135-1129	*Ramesses VII*
Third Intermediate Period	1070-713 BC		
		1070-945	Twenty-First Dynasty
		945-713	Twenty-Second Dynasty
		828-713	Twenty-Third Dynasty
		724-713	Twenty-Fourth Dynasty
Late Period	713-332 BC		
		713-656	Twenty-Fifth Dynasty (Kushite)
		690-664	*Taharka*
		664-525	Twenty-Sixth Dynasty (Saite)
		525-404	Twenty-Seventh Dynasty (Persian)
		404-399	Twenty-Eighth Dynasty
		399-380	Twenty-Ninth Dynasty
		380-343	Thirtieth Dynasty
		343-332	Thirty-First Dynasty (Persian)
Graeco-Roman Period	332 BC-AD 395		
		332-305	Macedonian Dynasty
		305-30	Ptolemaic Dynasty
		30 BC-AD 395	Roman Period

1
Introduction

As the ancient Egyptians had no direct equivalents to our modern words 'game' and 'sport', it is not possible to state with any degree of certainty which activities they themselves would have expected to find included in this book. Today a game can be defined, quite simply, as a pastime with rules that allow the determination of a winner; it is this ability to produce a winner that distinguishes a game from unstructured play. Physical activity is not an essential component of a game, but many games are physical, and games can depend on any combination of luck, skill or strength. A sport, in contrast, can be defined as a pastime that requires physical exertion. Many would wish to narrow this definition by insisting that a sport must have acknowledged rules and a scoring system that decides a winner. Others would exclude all activities that rely to a large extent on animals or machinery. It is obvious that there is an overlap between sport and games, with experts failing to agree on the classification of activities as diverse as archery, boxing, hunting, acrobatics and rowing – all activities enjoyed by the ancient Egyptians. And so I have here adopted the loosest of definitions, classifying sport and games as active pastimes governed by rules or customs. Following this definition, Egyptian dance, which cannot be meaningfully separated from acrobatics, is accepted as a sport.

All of Egypt's games, and many of her sports, were capable of producing a winner. Yet all archaeological and textual evidence indicates that sporting competition was virtually unknown. The king excepted, Egypt never developed the tradition of the individual sporting hero such as would play an important role in the development of Greek culture. There is no evidence for either organised team sport or individual competition as a regular, secular, public spectacle and, before the arrival of the Greeks, no exclusively sports-based architecture. The evidence is undoubtedly biased, concentrating as it does on Egypt's elite and coming almost entirely from funerary and ritual contexts, but it is clear that there was no equivalent of the Olympic Games or the modern football match to stir and unite a large crowd.

Played at the lowest, most informal level, games and sports had no obvious consequence beyond the generation of pleasure, peer bonding and the determination of a winner. Family or village games, important though they may have been to the participants, were ephemeral pleasures which, lacking any form of complicated equipment, have made little impact on the archaeological record. Higher up the social pyramid, sports served as social signifiers; elite men hunted in the marshes or practised archery alongside the king, not necessarily because they enjoyed the sporting life, but because these were the pursuits that an Egyptian gentleman should be seen to enjoy. Included on elite tomb walls, hunting scenes conveyed a message of everlasting prestige and virility. Meanwhile secular board games developed their own ritual meanings, until a game played against an invisible opponent became a recognised means of bridging the gulf between the living and the dead.

At the highest, most official level sport was a performance art. As such it was incorporated into religious and political rituals as a means of demonstrating the superiority of the Egyptian people and, most particularly, the Egyptian king. Kings rarely entered into open competition, but when they did the outcome was never in doubt. They, or their team, invariably won. This was both a tactful concession and an important theological point. From the very dawn of the dynastic age the king of Egypt was officially the strongest, bravest and most vigorous of men, and he used his athletic prowess to confirm his fitness to rule. To admit that the king could lose at anything would be to admit that *maat* – the concept of rightness, justice and status quo that underpinned the Egyptian kingship – could be overcome by chaos. To depict the king succeeding was to reinforce magically his ability to succeed. Given the importance of this message, it was perhaps inevitable that tests of skill and stamina would come to play an important part in the rites associated with renewal and kingship.

2

Board games

Egypt's elite tombs have yielded many beautifully crafted game sets, and there are additional representations of game boards, game pieces and game players on tomb walls dating from the Old Kingdom to the end of the Dynastic Age (figure 1). Board games were not, however, the sole preserve of the upper classes. Archaeology confirms that ephemeral boards could be scratched on to stone or in mud, while ethnology shows that modern game players often trace a simple board in Egypt's sands. With pebbles used as gaming pieces and animal knucklebones for dice, anyone, rich or poor, adult or child, could enjoy a board game. It is therefore frustrating that, in the absence of anything resembling a book of rules, it is impossible to state precisely how any of the evidently popular games were played.

All of Egypt's board games combined strategy with luck. Despite Howard Carter's assertion that he found three dice (two of clay and one of limestone) among Eighteenth Dynasty objects recovered from the rubbish heaps of the Deir el-Bahri temple, there is little evidence for the use of dice (cubes marked with the spotted numbers one to six; usually

1. First Dynasty label, probably from a container for gaming pieces, recovered from the tomb of King Djer at Abydos. (British Museum 35525)

with opposite faces totalling seven) until the Graeco-Roman Period. Instead, moves were determined either by the throw of casting sticks or by the throw of knucklebones (*astragali*).

In their most basic form the Egyptian casting sticks were short, flat sticks carved from wood or ivory, light (L) on one side and dark (D) on the other. The most elaborate examples, included among those recovered from Tutankhamun's tomb (KV 62), were carved with images of Nubian and Asiatic captives. When thrown, the sticks landed either light or dark side uppermost; a set of four casting sticks therefore gave a possible five combinations of faces (DDDD, DDDL, DDLL, DLLL, LLLL). The simplest scoring system used by modern game players employing throwing sticks assigns a numerical value of one to the dark face; this gives a range of possible scores from zero (no dark faces visible; occasionally this combination is given the score five) to four (all four dark faces uppermost).

Knucklebones, either genuine sheep bones or facsimiles carved from wood or ivory, had four distinct faces. In the classical world these faces were assigned a numeric value: one (flat side), three (concave side), four (convex side), six (twisted side). Throwing a pair of knucklebones and totalling the scores of the uppermost faces would give nine possible outcomes (two, four, five, six, seven, eight, nine, ten and twelve).

Senet

The most popular board game was *senet* ('the passing game', also known as 'thirty squares'), a game not dissimilar to our modern backgammon (figure 2). The earliest clear reference to *senet* playing is found in the Third Dynasty Saqqara tomb of the overseer of the royal scribes Hesy-Re, but occasional finds of playing pieces, game boards

2. Two men playing *senet* in the Old Kingdom tomb of Nebkauhor at Saqqara. (After Pusch 1979, pl. 6)

3. Restored wooden *senet* board displaying the tall, cone-shaped playing pieces and the shorter, reel-shaped pieces. (Cairo Museum)

and *senet* hieroglyphs suggest that the game was well established by the First Dynasty. The last known reference to *senet* dates to the third century AD.

Senet was a two-person game played on a rectangular board (average size 35–55 cm by 10–20 cm), bearing three parallel, adjoining rows of ten squares or 'houses'. Old Kingdom *senet* boards often had short legs in the shape of bulls' legs. Eighteenth and Nineteenth Dynasty *senet* sets took the form of elaborate drawered boxes carved from wood or ivory and inlaid with ebony, ivory and faience. The upper surface of the box served as the gaming board while the drawer beneath, held shut by a wooden or metal bolt, housed both the playing pieces and the casting sticks or knucklebones. These early New Kingdom *senet* boxes often stood on a purpose-made stand or table. By the Twentieth Dynasty *senet* was again being played on a slab board manufactured from stone, wood or faience.

Tomb illustrations show that each player had either seven (Old Kingdom) or five (New Kingdom) wooden, ivory or faience playing pieces known as 'dancers' (*ibau*), either tall and cone-shaped or shorter and reel-shaped (figure 3). The object of the game was to guide all the dancers through all the houses on the board, reversing direction on every row, and blocking, diverting and passing over the opponent's pieces wherever possible. The final five houses were the most important, as they allowed the pieces to complete and exit the game.

Occasional inscribed houses – the ancient equivalent of the 'snakes' and 'ladders' in our modern game – made the journey around the board more exciting. During the New Kingdom 'the frog' (square 15 or 'the house of rebirth') was a lucky square. The neighbouring 'netting' square, square 16, was unlucky. Square 27, a flooded field representing the waters of chaos, was the unluckiest of all; here the unwary might drown, their playing piece being removed from the board. During the Old and Middle Kingdoms the final five houses carried a practical message: 'good, bad, three, two, one' (the three-two-one sequence being

4. Late New Kingdom faience *senet* board fragment from Tanis, showing the final five houses and their gods. (Cairo 88007)

considered particularly propitious). During the New Kingdom they developed a more mystical significance, as the simple numbers became three, two and one gods (figure 4).

While *senet* remained a popular secular pastime throughout the dynastic age, the underlying symbolism of the game evolved as ideas of the afterlife developed. The earliest tomb-wall images, which are included among scenes of daily life, appear to show a simple leisure activity with two living opponents playing while the deceased stands by and watches (figure 5). By the Sixth Dynasty the deceased has abandoned

5. *Senet* players in the Middle Kingdom tomb of Kheti at Beni Hasan. Here *senet* is included among the many daily activities performed by the living. (After Newberry 1893, pl. 13)

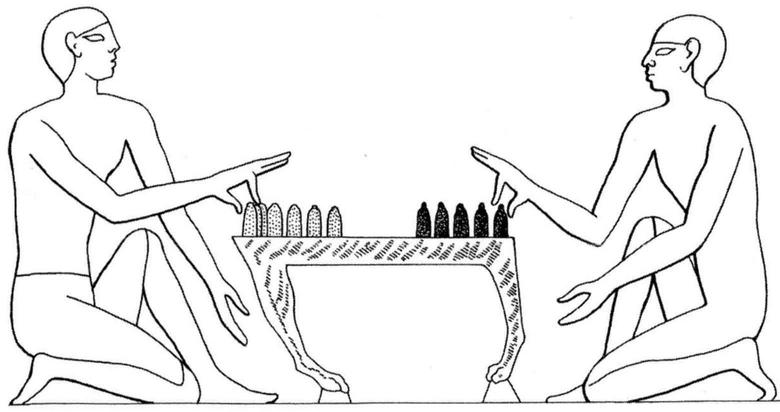

the passive role to sit at the board and play a living opponent. Already, it seems, the game is a conduit that allows the dead to communicate with the living.

During the New Kingdom the deceased is often shown playing an invisible opponent, who may be identified either as Death or as his own soul. *Senet* has become equated with the idea of resurrection and the struggle of the soul of the deceased to reach the security of eternal life. By the Nineteenth Dynasty *senet*-playing scenes are frequently used to illustrate the *Chapters of Coming Forth by Day* (*Book of the Dead*), Chapter 17. It is now considered prudent for even non-players to include a *senet* set among the standard grave goods. *Senet* sets manufactured purely for inclusion in the tomb may be identified by their inscriptions; the *senet* set portrayed in the Nineteenth Dynasty tomb of Sennefer (TT 96B), for example, bears the formula 'An offering which the king makes to Amun-Re, King of the Gods, that he might give life, prosperity, health and alertness before the Lord of the Two Lands for the Ka [spirit] of the mayor, Sennefer, justified'. A few Twentieth Dynasty *senet* sets have religious inscriptions on every square and were also, it is assumed, designed for purely ritual use.

Twenty-squares

Similar to *senet* was the simpler game of 'twenty-squares', a Near Eastern board game brought to Egypt by the Hyksos during the Second Intermediate Period. Twenty-squares quickly became popular and, from the Eighteenth Dynasty onwards, playing boards were regularly

6. A twenty-squares box and tokens, and a separate pair of casting sticks, both recovered from Tutankhamun's tomb. (Cairo Museum)

incorporated into the base of *senet* boxes. The twenty 'squares' (which were more often than not oblong) were arranged in three parallel rows of four, twelve, four, with every fourth square on the long row marked with a rosette or hieroglyph (figure 6). The game was played by two players with five tokens each.

Mehen

Mehen is the name of the coiled snake god who protects the sun god Re as he passes through the dark, dangerous night of the Underworld. *Mehen*, 'the snake game', was popular during the Predynastic Period and Old Kingdom but disappeared from Egypt at the end of the First Intermediate Period. Some Twenty-Sixth Dynasty Egyptian tomb walls, deliberately archaic in their decoration, include *mehen* scenes, but there is no evidence to suggest that the game was once again being played. Whether it had been prohibited for religious reasons or had merely fallen out of fashion is not now clear. The earliest mention of the *mehen* game in a religious context is found in the Old Kingdom *Pyramid Texts*, where the deceased is required to travel around the board, from the serpent's tail to its head. The first written references to the 'Mysteries of Mehen' (*Coffin Text* Spells 493 and 495), the spiralling 'Roads of Mehen' (Spells 758–760) and the 'Coiled One' as the guardian of the sun (Spells 758, 759) date to the Middle Kingdom and so coincide with the disappearance of the game.

Mehen was played on a circular stone or wooden board whose upper surface was shaped like a coiled snake with regular scale-like slots carved along its back (figures 7, 8). On some boards the tail of

7. (Right) Limestone *mehen* board and playing pieces. (British Museum)

8. (Below) *Senet* and *mehen*; part of a larger scene showing wrestling, stick fighting, music (pictured) and dance, all performed in honour of Hathor. From the Sixth Dynasty tomb of Idu at Saqqara. (After Simpson 1976, pl. 38)

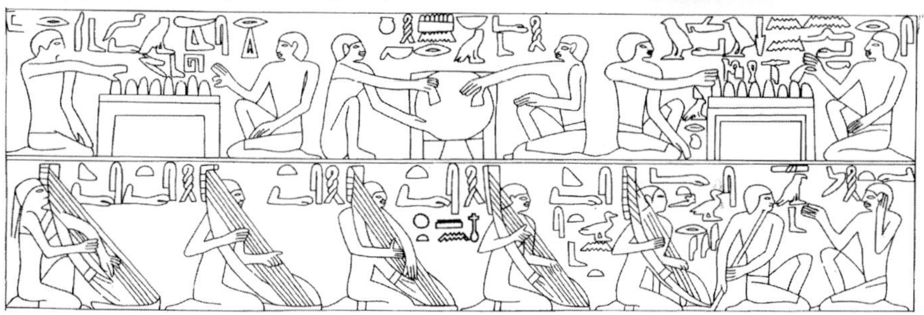

the snake, assumed to be the starting point of the game, was shaped like a duck's head. There was no standard number of slots (boards range from fewer than thirty slots to over three hundred) and no specific direction of play; both clockwise and counter-clockwise examples are known. Nor was there a standard size; a miniature limestone *mehen* board (a travelling version?) was recovered from the prehistoric Ballas cemetery (Grave Q19: Ashmolean Museum, Oxford), where it was employed as the lid of a pot.

The unusual painted walls of Hesy-Re's tomb display his games equipment: a *senet* board and accessories including *senet* playing pieces, a *mehen* board, an assortment of marbles, three lion and three lioness tokens or playing pieces and a set of four casting sticks (figure 9). Hesy-Re's *mehen* board was a seven-coiled serpent with up to four hundred slots, whose head, initial coil and tail retained some of their original paintwork, showing that the snake was once black with yellow streaks. It seems obvious that the object of the game was to race a token or tokens around the snake, working inwards towards the head, with moves being determined either by casting sticks or by guessing the number of marbles held in an opponent's hand. However, it is not obvious which tokens were used. Were the lions and lionesses, conveniently housed in a nearby box, raced around the board (figures 10, 11)? Or were the marbles, stored in the same box, dropped into the slots?

9. Board games, including a *mehen* board, *senet* board and *men* board plus playing pieces, casting sticks and marbles, illustrated on the walls of the Third Dynasty tomb of Hesy-Re at Saqqara. (After Quibell 1913)

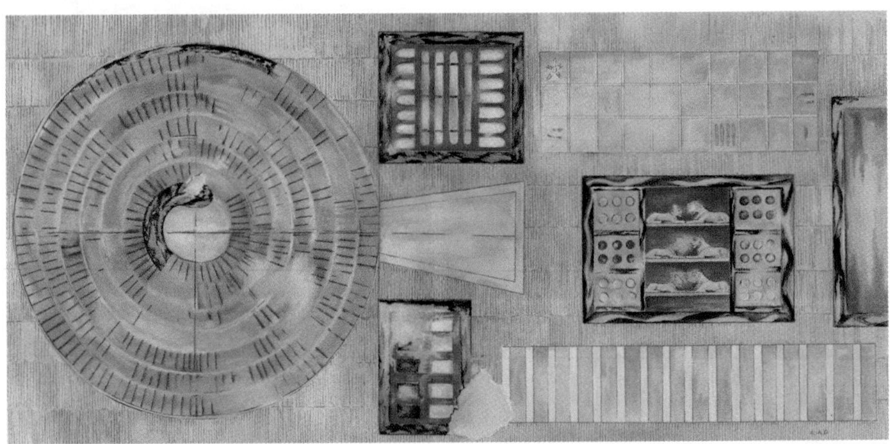

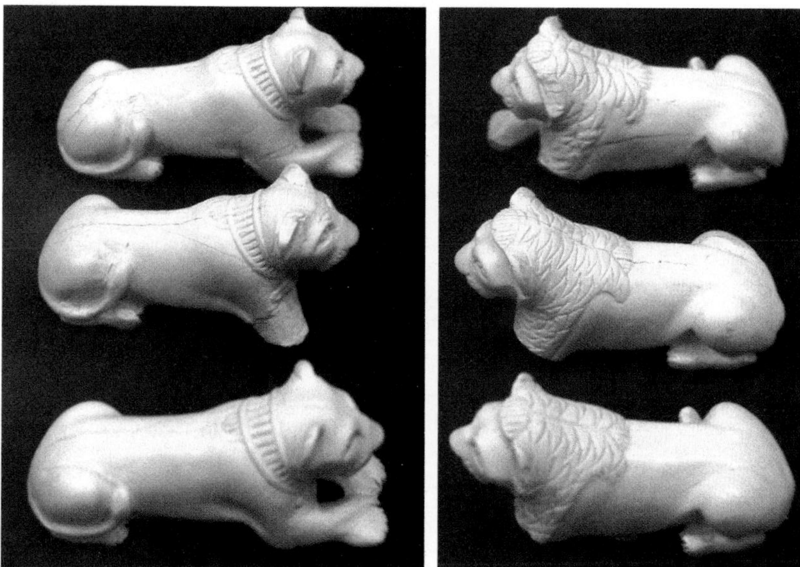

10. (Above left) Ivory game pieces in the form of lionesses. (Cairo Museum)

11. (Above right) Ivory game pieces in the form of lions. (Cairo Museum)

Men

Men ('endurance'), again a game for two, was played on a long board divided into thirteen or more sections. Each player had five pieces that they raced along the board, the moves being determined by either casting sticks or knucklebones. This game was popular during the First Dynasty but had disappeared by the middle of the Old Kingdom. Hesy-Re's *men* board was striped with sixteen narrow bands of yellow and sixteen broader bands of a deeper yellow with red outlines. The oblong playing pieces, five black and five white, were stored in a nearby box.

Dogs and jackals

During the First Intermediate Period a variant of *men*, using pegs rather than pieces, was played throughout the Near East. The best surviving Egyptian board is that discovered by Howard Carter in the Twelfth Dynasty tomb of Reny-Seneb at Deir el-Bahri (pit tomb 25) and originally identified as an axe-shaped ivory box with ten very beautiful hairpins – five with jackal heads and five with dog heads. Soon after, Carter realised that the 'box' was actually a playing board and that

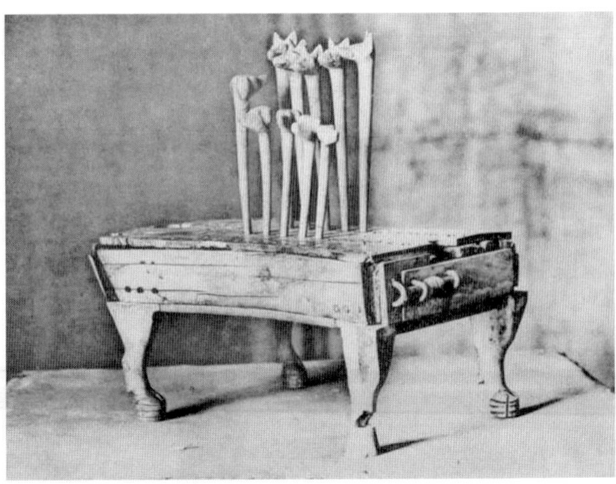

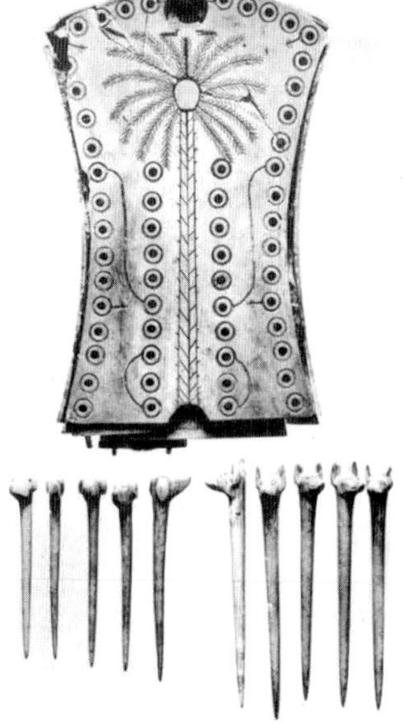

12. (Above and left) Dogs and jackals board and ivory game pieces, recovered from the Twelfth Dynasty tomb of Reny-Seneb at Deir el-Bahri. (After Carnarvon and Carter 1912, pl. 50)

the 'hairpins' were the playing pegs. He called the new game 'dogs contra jackals' (figure 12).

Made of ivory, ebony and sycamore wood, Reny-Seneb's box is shield-shaped and symmetrical, measuring 15 by 10 cm (maximum dimensions) and standing just 7 cm tall on ivory bull's legs. A drawer under the gaming board fastens with an ivory bolt. The playing surface, made from two ivory sheets, has thirty holes for each player: one shared central hole taking the form of a *shen* sign signifying totality, nineteen holes running along the outer edge of the board and ten leading up the centre. The middle of the board is decorated with a palm-tree design. The aim of the game was apparently to move the five pegs along the holes, and it seems likely that, having started at the heart of the palm tree, the winner would be the first player to place all five pegs in the end holes (holes 25–29) either side of the *shen* hole. Lines connecting holes 6 and 20 and holes 8 and 10 may have been short cuts or diversions; the *nefer*, or 'good' sign, displayed at holes 15 and 25 probably indicated a safe haven. Moves were presumably dictated by knucklebones or casting sticks.

A simpler, far cheaper pottery version of the dogs and jackals board was recovered by Flinders Petrie at the Middle Kingdom pyramid village of Kahun. Lacking the elaborate legs and drawer, and minus the palm tree, it retains the shield shape and offers the same twenty-nine holes per player, and the same short cuts and *nefer* signs.

3

Non-board games

Games requiring little or no equipment – memory games, story-telling games, guessing games and many gambling games, for example – enjoy a timeless, worldwide popularity with both adults and children, yet leave no trace in the archaeological record. It therefore seems prudent to assume that the games that have survived are just a fraction (albeit maybe a large fraction) of the games actually played.

Ball games

Egyptian balls were solid, made from spheres of wood or clay, from sewn leather or linen (figure 13) stuffed with barley husks, rags and chopped dried grass, or from strips of papyrus or plaited palm leaf wound round and round just as we today wind a ball of string (figure 14). They ranged in size between 3 and 9 cm in diameter and were, in comparison with modern air-filled balls, heavy to handle. More fragile hollow faience spheres have been recovered from tombs, but it seems highly unlikely that these delicate, expensive objects would have been used to play vigorous games.

13. A sewn ball which has burst open to reveal the stuffing inside. (Manchester Museum 96)

Tomb scenes rarely show children playing informally with balls although it seems inconceivable, given the number of surviving examples, that they did not. Ball games were included among the scenes of daily life used to decorate the Middle Kingdom

14. Ball made from woven papyrus fibres. (Cairo Museum 68150)

15. 'Piggy-back' catch played in the Middle Kingdom tomb of Baqet III at Beni Hasan. The game appears on the north wall of the main chamber alongside images of typical female activities – women spinning and weaving, and girls dancing, juggling and playing with their friends. (Photograph: Angela Thomas)

rock-cut tombs of the provincial dignitaries at Beni Hasan. In the tombs of Baqet III (Tomb 15) and Kheti (Tomb 17) girls, who may be distinguished from the more mature but identically sized women by their braided and weighted hair, juggle and play team games of catching and throwing. The most athletic ball game is a form of 'piggy-back' catch, where the thrower, apparently unhindered by her calf-length sheath dress, sits on her friend's back (figure 15). It seems likely that a dropped ball resulted in the thrower and her carrier changing positions.

Catching and throwing appear to have been exclusively female skills. Boys preferred to hit balls with sticks. In Kheti's tomb young men are shown playing a hockey-like game, controlling what appears to be a small wooden hoop with bent-ended sticks. However, given the conventions and limitations of Egyptian art, it is not certain whether this 'hoop' should be interpreted as a hoop, a disk or a solid ball.

A more formal bat and ball 'game' – the ritual of 'striking the ball' – makes its first appearance during the Eighteenth Dynasty reign of Tuthmosis III, although *Pyramid Text* Spell 254, which instructs the deceased to 'strike the ball on the meadow of Hapi', suggests that it

16. Amenhotep III performs the 'striking the ball' ritual before Hathor (or, as the goddess is unnamed, perhaps Mut) at the Luxor temple. (After Decker and Herb 1994, pl. 62)

might have originated during the Old Kingdom, possibly evolving from an entirely secular game. The ritual, recorded on temple walls and played by the king in the presence of a goddess (usually Hathor, but occasionally Mut, Tefnut or Sekhmet), required the king to hit a ball with a stick (either bent, straight or club-like) so that he might symbolically destroy the evil eye of the snake god Apophis.

At Deir el-Bahri Tuthmosis stands before Hathor, kilted and wearing the *atef* crown. He holds a curious undulating stick in his right hand. Two smaller-scale priests face the king, each holding a ball; an accompanying text explains that they are to field the balls. Amenhotep III, 'striking the ball' at the Luxor temple, has no attendant priests (figure 16). He uses a straight stick, again held in the right hand; the large ball held in his left hand suggests that the stick is to be used one-handed. This ritual vanished during the reign of Akhenaten, only to reappear on the walls of the Ptolemaic Period temples of Edfu, Dendera and Philae. One other ball ritual, known only from the time of the Late Period king Taharka, involved throwing four balls towards the four points of the compass (or the four winds) while running. This ceremony is illustrated at Karnak.

Kahun, one of the few Egyptian domestic sites to have survived for excavation, yielded at least eleven short, shaped wooden sticks, which

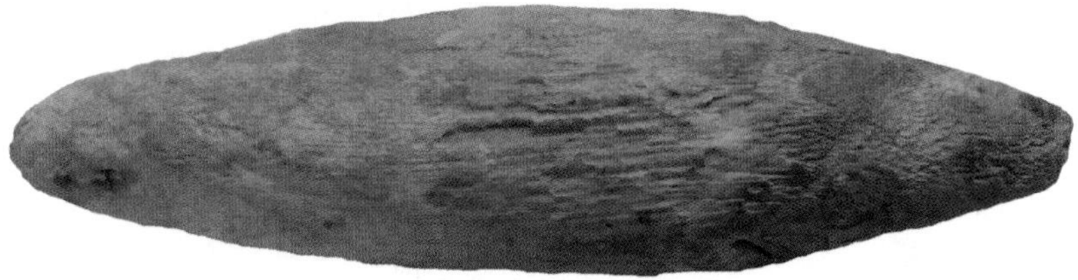

17. Wooden tipcat recovered by Flinders Petrie from Kahun. (Manchester Museum 86)

Flinders Petrie identified as the 'cats' used in an ancient version of the traditional British game variously known as 'tipcat' (South), 'nipsy' (Yorkshire) or 'piggy' (Lancashire) – a game that, despite its quaint name, was taken seriously and was played regularly both by children and adults, often for money, until the mid twentieth century (figure 17). In the modern version of the game a hard piece of wood, the 'cat' or 'piggy' (often the knot out of a railway sleeper), is laid across a flat stone or brick and then 'risen' – hit with a stick, pick handle or bat – so that it flies up into the air. The airborne cat is then struck with the stick; the cat that travels the furthest wins.

Marbles – small solid balls of clay, faience or stone – were included amongst Hesy-Re's games equipment. They had a variety of potential uses: as amusements in their own right; as games pieces; as gambling tokens, with opponents challenging each other to guess the number of marbles held in a clenched fist; as bowling balls in miniature games of skittles. In the prehistoric Naqada cemetery, the fill from a large but regrettably plundered child's grave (Grave 100) yielded a set of nine small vase-shaped skittles carved from limestone and red and white breccia, four diorite marbles each less than 1.5 cm in diameter and three marble blocks which could be assembled into a gate or arch with a 2.6 cm span, through which, it is presumed, the marbles had to be rolled. Today this equipment is displayed in the Ashmolean Museum, Oxford. Grave 1215 in the same cemetery included sixteen balls, one gate block and a series of ivory throwing sticks; Graves 1229 and 373 also yielded components of the skittle game. Other Naqada graves included a variety of games equipment including a pottery game table marked with painted red squares, marbles and gaming pieces shaped like lions and hares.

Children's games and sports

Few of Egypt's children attended school. Those who did were faced with a curriculum that focused on the reading, writing and mathematical skills needed to become an efficient scribe. There may, however, have been some form of physical education. The New Kingdom *Tale of Truth and Falsehood* tells us how a young boy, the hero of the tale, 'was sent to school, where he learned to write very well. He practised all the arts of war and surpassed his older companions.' Textual evidence indicates that children were taught to swim, and elite boys were also taught the essential social skills of hunting, shooting, fishing and, from the New Kingdom onwards, chariotry. It seems reasonable to assume that those who did not attend school received vocational training, with, for example, male army recruits being given exercises to make them fit, and dancers of both sexes being trained in the intricacies of their art.

The Greek historian Diodorus Siculus, writing during the first century BC and heavily influenced by his own cultural heritage, tells the unlikely story of the father of the legendary Egyptian king Sesoosis, who decided that his son, and all boys born on the same day, should be raised according to strict and suspiciously Greek principles:

> He trained the boys by a regime of unremitting exercises and hardships, and not one of them was allowed to have anything to eat unless he had first run one hundred and eighty stades [approximately 20 miles or 32 km]. As a result, as they reached manhood, they all had athletic bodies and a strong sense of leadership....
>
> (Diodorus Siculus *Library of History* 1:53)

More credibly, Old and Middle Kingdom tomb walls reveal children (usually identified by their 'sidelock of youth' hairstyle) enjoying a variety of physical activities, with boys and girls, for the most part, playing separately. Without any real understanding of why these scenes were chosen for inclusion in the tomb it is difficult to assess how typical, and how spontaneous, these games might be. In many cases it is impossible to determine what exactly is happening; it has been suggested, in the case of the boys at least, that some of the scenes might represent rites of passage. By the Ramesside Period the principles of tomb decoration had altered and, with more emphasis on religious scenes, we lose sight of the playful children.

If we take the scenes at face value, as representations of daily life, we see young women dancing, juggling and practising their acrobatics while young men favour jumping games, tests of strength and balance (boys carrying each other; boys weightlifting with heavy bags) and ropeless tugs of war. In the tomb of Baqet III young men and women together play the whirling or star game apparently known to the Egyptians as 'erecting the wine-arbour' – a game that is popular in playgrounds throughout the world today (figure 18). The players, as many as six at

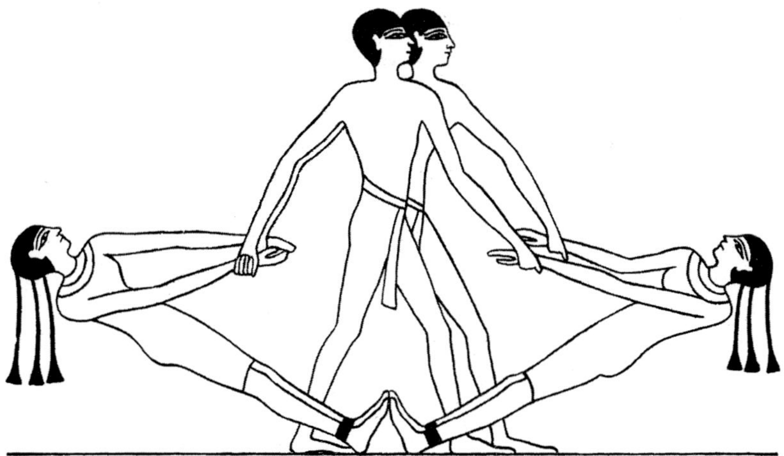

18. Boys and girls together play the whirling game in the tomb of Baqet III. (After Newberry 1893, pl. 4)

a time, hold hands, rock backwards on their heels and are spun round as fast as possible until they become breathless and dizzy. This game is also found in the Old Kingdom tombs of Ptahhotep (played by boys only) and Mereruka (girls only).

The Old Kingdom tombs of Ptahhotep and Idu and the Middle Kingdom tomb of Baqet III show boys playing what appears to be a throwing game (figure 19). Long, pointed sticks are thrown overarm

19. Boys playing the stick game on the south wall of the main chamber of the tomb of Baqet III. The next scene shows boys apparently competing to lift heavy bags. (After Newberry 1893, pl. 7)

into, and must stick upright in, either a raised target or a target zone scratched on the ground.

Toys

The Naqada cemetery yielded a series of stone macehead-like objects, made of soft stone and painted with bold black designs. Petrie, suspecting that he had discovered prehistoric spinning tops, made copies out of cardboard and spun them, producing a pleasing, flickering effect. The spinning top would remain popular throughout the dynastic age: Middle Kingdom Kahun yielded twenty roughly carved wooden spinning tops, while more elaborate faience versions date to the Roman Period.

Miniature figures present the archaeologist with a problem. Are they children's playthings, or are they models with a now-lost symbolic or religious meaning? All too often it is the context of a discovery that offers the only clue to its original purpose. Doll-like figures recovered from adult graves, often with an emphasised pubic region, are assumed to be concubine or fertility figurines intended to encourage rebirth and sexual potency after death (figure 20). Rag dolls and dolls with movable limbs recovered from children's graves or domestic sites are classified as toys. The more sophisticated of these dolls were made of painted wood with jointed arms and legs, wigs of hair or mud beads and collections of miniature clothes. In a room in one of the houses at Kahun, Petrie (1890:30) discovered bundles of hair, apparently waiting to be implanted into small wooden heads: 'This hair is constructed just like that made for Theban dolls; five threads placed together, about 6 inches [15 cm] long, had pellets of mud rolled on them by the fingers, 12 or 14 in the length, and a conical lump at the end.'

Small clay animals, including crocodiles, hippopotami, monkeys, cattle and donkeys, have been recovered from sites of various ages.

20. Wooden paddle 'doll' with realistic hair and a patterned dress. The emphasised pubic triangle suggests that this is a fertility figurine rather than a child's plaything. (Cairo Museum 56274)

Again, it can be difficult to distinguish genuine toys from votive offerings or funerary models, but a herd of small animals recovered from Kahun can be classified as toys; the collection, which includes a pig, a hippopotamus, a crocodile, an ape, a man and a boat, testifies to the popularity of clay as a children's modelling material. Less convincing is the excavator's identification of a thin flint flake chipped into the shape of a hippopotamus as a toy; flint, being both extremely brittle and extremely sharp, is an unsuitable material for toy manufacture in even the least safety-conscious of cultures.

More sophisticated wooden animals were given hinged moving parts manipulated by string, so that a crocodile might snap its lower jaw (Berlin Museum), a cat might yawn (figure 21) or a mouse might squeak (British Museum). Occasionally wheels were added to the toys, with the best wheeled animals dating to the Roman Period. Speculation that a streamlined Ptolemaic wooden bird recovered from Saqqara (Cairo Museum 22.6347) might have been designed to fly will remain, until the piece can be tested, mere speculation. The most splendid example of the toymaker's art comes from the Middle Kingdom Lisht cemetery and is now housed in Cairo Museum. Three naked ivory pygmies stand

21. New Kingdom wooden cat recovered from Thebes. The mouth can be made to close by pulling on the string. (British Museum 15671)

22. Three dancing pygmies, part of a set of four, recovered from the Middle Kingdom Lisht cemetery. (Cairo Museum 63858)

on a round base, their arms raised as they prepare to dance (figure 22). A fourth pygmy (now separated from the dancers and housed in New York) stands ready to clap out a rhythm. Strings attached to the figures pass through a box and into the hands of the child, who, by pulling the strings, can control the dancers.

4

Athletics

With the exception of the Eighteenth Dynasty Akhenaten, who was happy to be depicted with a sagging, feminised body, Egypt's kings were invariably depicted as fit and healthy individuals. The New Kingdom monarchs in particular placed great emphasis on their own physical prowess. Siptah was so determined to conform to this stereotype that the royal artists ignored his twisted leg; the female pharaoh Hatshepsut had herself depicted with a man's body.

The royal run

Amenhotep II, arguably the most athletic of the sporting kings, raised a stela at Giza (known today as the Sphinx Stela) to commemorate his own all-round abilities, which included archery, running, rowing and riding.

This was no vain or meaningless boast. The health of the king could be equated with the health of the country, and from earliest times Egypt's kings were expected to perform athletic feats, before an elite audience, which would prove their fitness to rule (figure 23). The Circuit of the Walls – an archaic ceremony mentioned on the Old Kingdom Palermo

23. The Early Dynastic Narmer Macehead. The scene illustrated was originally identified as a wedding ceremony, and subsequently as a *heb sed* celebration, but it is now recognised that the macehead depicts ceremonial activities concerned with kingship and renewal. In the centre of the illustration three bearded runners race between a set of curved, triple D-shaped markers. (Ashmolean Museum)

Stone – evolved into a walk or run around the walls of the northern capital, Memphis. The Running of the Apis Bull may have involved both king and bull circling Memphis. Better known is the *heb sed* or jubilee celebration, a ceremony of renewal or rejuvenation performed – in theory – by individual kings after thirty years on the throne and every three years thereafter, although many kings chose to celebrate well before their thirtieth year. The *heb sed* included a ritual run in which the king raced against an invisible but deadly enemy – old age.

Although the underlying principle of the *heb sed* is well understood, the ceremony itself is ill documented. The earliest evidence for the *heb sed* race comes from the Abydos tomb of the First Dynasty king Den, which has yielded a wooden label and a seal, both showing the king running. Better evidence comes from the Third Dynasty Saqqara Step Pyramid complex, a complex that re-created in stone many aspects of King Djoser's mud-brick palace so that his spirit might perform the rituals of kingship for all eternity. Here a 140 metre long track in the south courtyard allowed Djoser's spirit to run around two curved double-D shaped markers, which, stretching from north to south, may have represented the boundaries of his power – either Upper and Lower Egypt, or heaven and earth (figure 24). The shape of the markers is curious; when illustrated, *heb sed* markers are invariably shown as triple rather than double-D shapes. Beneath Djoser's pyramid, in the 'King's Apartment', the blue tile-lined walls (blue being the colour of regeneration) include two scenes showing the king running

24. The *heb sed* court in front of Djoser's Saqqara Step Pyramid.

25. Amenhotep III runs towards the goddess Mut, carrying a mace and sceptre. Luxor temple. (After Decker and Herb 1994, pl. 23)

his *heb sed* race. In one the king, dressed in a brief loincloth, clutches a flail and the scroll that (we imagine) states his right to rule. In the second scene the king wears a penis sheath.

Just three New Kingdom monarchs (Tuthmosis III, Amenophis III and Ramesses II) enjoyed more than thirty years on the throne but many more celebrated jubilees, and the stone temple walls have preserved several images of kings running in ceremonial races (figures 25, 26). It is, however, likely that at least some of these kings employed substitute runners to perform on their behalf.

Non-royal running

Running was an important aspect of military life. Couriers ran along desert paths to deliver urgent messages and, as scenes from the Amarna elite tombs

26. Hatshepsut runs on the wall of the Red Chapel, Karnak temple. Running is normally a male activity, but as a female pharaoh Hatshepsut is forced to perform male rituals.

confirm, bodyguards ran alongside royal chariots, providing a questionable level of protection for their king. It therefore seems likely that regular runs were included in routine army training. It may also be that running was popular away from the barracks, but running as a sport or leisure activity leaves no trace in the archaeological record and we do not read of our first official race until the Late Period reign of Taharka, when the Dahshur Running Stela (685 BC) preserves details of a race by army units who ran from Memphis across the desert to the Faiyum and back – an impressive 65 miles (105 km). Watched by the king, who provided prizes for the winners and runners-up, and who even joined the runners for a short distance, the victor covered the first part of the run in four hours. Sports historian Wolfgang Decker (1992, 62–6) has estimated that, allowing for a two-hour rest in the Faiyum, the entire run was completed in eleven hours – four hours for the first leg, and five for the second.

Jumping

Evidence for other forms of athletics is scanty in the extreme. However, the idea of a jumping competition as a means of identifying the fittest was by no means unknown, and an Eighteenth/Nineteenth Dynasty fantasy, *The Tale of the Doomed Prince*, tells how the King of Naharin locked his beautiful and very desirable daughter in a high tower:

> And here at the window the beautiful princess stood alone, looking down on the world below. The King of Naharin summoned her noble suitors to the base of the tower. All the unmarried princes of Syria arrived at the tower and listened as the King of Naharin spoke: 'Whoever jumps up to my daughter's window, he will win her hand in marriage.' The princes immediately started to leap upwards, competing to reach the window. They did this day after day, for they were each determined to win the hand of the beautiful princess.

Naturally, the winner turned out to be a prince of Egypt!

While jumping played a part in dance and acrobatics, there is no further evidence for adult jumping – either long jump or high jump – as a sport. Children, however, did jump. Middle Kingdom girls jump in the Beni Hasan tombs, and a children's jumping game is featured in the Old Kingdom Saqqara tombs of Ptahhotep and Mereruka (figure 27). Here we see a pair of naked boys sitting on the ground, legs and arms outstretched, the heel of one foot resting on the toe of the other and one hand placed above the other. The boys are shown one above the other, sitting on different registers, but comparison with the modern adult jumping game *khazza iawizza,* which is still played in the Middle East today, suggests that they should actually be envisaged as sitting opposite each other, fingers and toes touching. Equally naked boys (one in the tomb of Ptahhotep; three in the tomb of Mereruka) compete by leaping over the human hurdle. In the tomb of Mereruka the lead boy

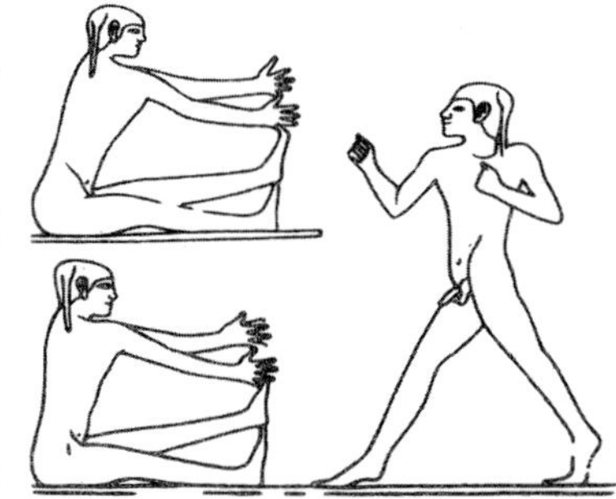

27. Jumping game in the Saqqara tomb of Ptah-hotep. The seated boys probably faced each other so that they formed a hurdle for their companion. (After Decker 1992, pl. 32)

shouts to his friends: 'Sit tight, here I come, friend!'

Pole climbing

Pole climbing – a ritual rather than a sport – was associated with the cult of the fertility god Min and was performed in the presence of the god. Representations dating from the Old to the New Kingdoms show four flimsy climbing posts propped steeply against a scarcely more sturdy central post. Ropes attached to the posts are pulled by teams of men; it is not clear whether the men are steadying the posts or causing them to sway to make the climb more difficult. The climbers, who appear to be racing to the top, wear feathers in their hair and are possibly intended to be either Libyans or, more likely, Nubians (figure 28).

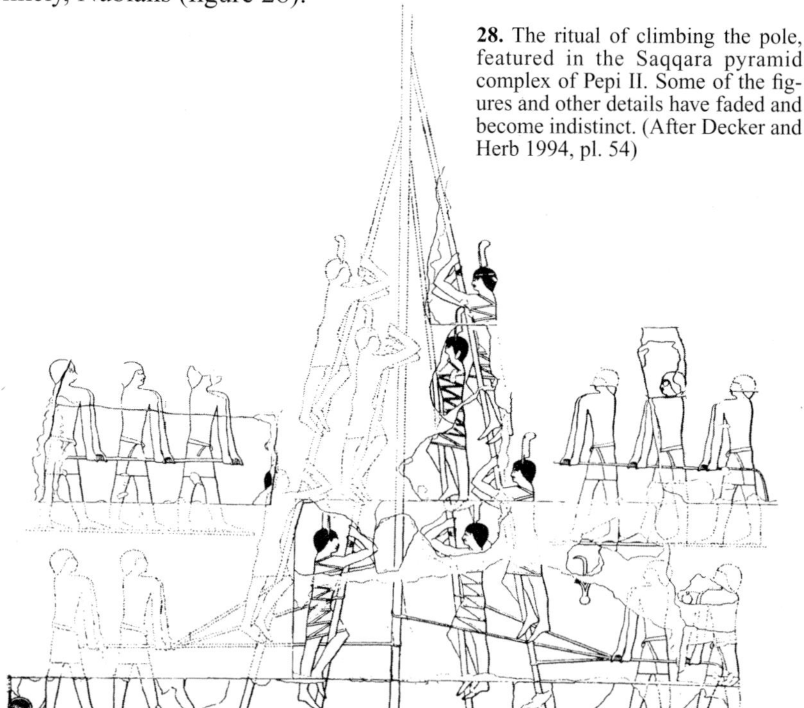

28. The ritual of climbing the pole, featured in the Saqqara pyramid complex of Pepi II. Some of the figures and other details have faded and become indistinct. (After Decker and Herb 1994, pl. 54)

5

Hunting, shooting and fishing

The first Egyptians were Palaeolithic nomads who lived in small bands and obtained their food through their hunting and gathering skills. Ethnology suggests that the gathered food (plants and small game) may have made the larger calorific contribution to the diet, but that the hunted food (meat) was the prestige item. The Neolithic brought agriculture, settlement and a hierarchical society to Egypt. Big-game hunting was no longer economically important, but respect for the fearless hunter persisted (figure 29). Naqada I decorated pottery reveals these prehistoric hunters as faceless stick-men who use harpoons and bows to hunt their prey, while just one Naqada II painted tomb (Tomb 100 at Hierakonpolis)

29. Hunting elephant in Predynastic Egypt. Naqada I image from Wadi Menhi, Wadi Hammamat. (After Decker and Herb 1994, pl. 130)

30. The Narmer Palette from Hierakonpolis. On the recto (shown left) Narmer smites his enemies. On the verso (shown right) the king marches in triumph before his defeated foes and takes the form of a bull to gore his enemies. (Cairo Museum CG14716)

survived to show, on its pale plaster walls, images of a calm river whose banks team with aggressive life: wild animals, valiant hunters, fighting and dying men.

Two centuries later, the association of animals, hunting and fighting with elite power is evident in a series of carved stone palettes, including the Narmer Palette, a ritual artefact that may be read as an unequivocal declaration of royal dominance: the bringing of *maat* (control) to chaos (figure 30). Egyptians from all walks of life still hunted small game, birds and fish to supplement their diet. But the hunting of dangerous, large animals had evolved into a prestige sport imbued with a deep significance; it seems that the hunter – invariably male – who killed a large animal was believed to absorb part of that animal's savage spirit, and successive kings used real or imaginary victories in the hunting field to confirm their physical and spiritual superiority over the disorganised and dangerous natural world.

Royal hunts

Egypt's flat deserts offered an exciting range of game: lion, leopard, ostrich, antelope, deer and gazelle. The animals were hunted by trapping or, more usually, by ambush, with lines of hunters, beaters and hounds making a noisy, co-ordinated advance on foot to drive their prey into a fenced area where they could then be dispatched with little risk to the huntsmen. There was no official hunting season, although the fact that many hunting scenes feature young animals indicates that hunting was primarily a spring sport.

The Old and Middle Kingdom hunters had access to a basic but effective armoury: the simple or self bow made from a single piece of wood; arrows made from reeds tipped with flint or wood; wooden spears, sticks, clubs, axes, slings and lassos. Targets were used for archery practice, but tomb images dating to the earlier part of the Old Kingdom suggest that only the king hunted with a bow and arrow, and that he alone, though assisted by an assortment of beaters, dogs and dog handlers (figure 31), and watched by his court, hunted large game. The accuracy and interpretation of these images has to be questioned. Are we looking at a genuine leisure activity or at symbolic representations of kingship – performances designed to reinforce the king's right to rule? Royal scenes can never be taken at face value, and we should perhaps remember that the Ptolemaic kings were happy to be depicted 'spearing the tortoise of Re', not because they enjoyed the thrills of a tortoise hunt but because in their mythological hunting scenes the tortoise – like the serpent, the oryx, the Seth animal and all kinds of foreigners – symbolised chaos.

31. Fifth Dynasty huntsman with dogs. From the Saqqara tomb of Ptahhotep. (After Davies 1900, pl. 22)

The first image of non-royal hunters participating in, rather than simply observing, the hunt comes from the Fifth Dynasty Saqqara tomb of Niankhkhnum and Khnumhotep, which also features scenes of fishing and bird hunting. The first image of a non-royal person hunting with bows and arrows comes from the First Intermediate Period tomb of Ankhtifi at Moalla; here, in the absence of an acknowledged king, the powerful local governor Ankhtifi claims his own royal privileges. On the wall to the right of the tomb entrance we see him spearing fish (figure 32). The scene on the opposite wall is now totally destroyed but, given

32. The First Intermediate Period nomarch Ankhtifi spears a fish on the wall of his Moalla tomb.

the Egyptian love of symmetry, may well have shown him hunting game. The back wall of the tomb shows a procession of men armed with bows and arrows and accompanied by hunting dogs.

With the restoration of national unity at the start of the Middle Kingdom hunting became a more egalitarian sport, with kings seemingly happy to hunt alongside their courtiers.

Archery and chariots

The New Kingdom hunters benefited from two Hyksos innovations. The light, two-wheeled horse-drawn chariot allowed the elite to race across the flat desert chasing their prey while loosing off a hail of arrows and spears. Suddenly ostrich hunting – so difficult on foot – was in vogue, while lion hunting became the sport of kings. The composite bow was made by gluing horn and sinew to a wooden simple bow. The result was a more elastic weapon of considerably improved range, accuracy and power. Now archery competitions offered yet another means of proving fitness to rule. But rather than compete against a living opponent, kings competed against their forebears, striving to beat their records. Tuthmosis III started this tradition by boasting of his own extraordinary prowess:

> ... when he shot at the target the wood splintered like papyrus. His Majesty dedicated an example of this in the temple of Amen, a target of worked copper three fingers thick, with an arrow in it after he had hit it and penetrated three hands' breadth through it , so that his descendants should desire the strength of his arm in bravery and power…
>
> (Armant Stela of Tuthmosis III. Touny and Wenig 1969: 35–6)

Tuthmosis' son and successor, Amenhotep II, studied archery as a boy under the acknowledged expert Min of Thinis. Illustrations in Min's Theban tomb (TT 109) show a lesson in progress – Amenhotep shoots into a large rectangular target and his arrows stick in place – while the broken text preserves some of Min's instructions: 'Stretch your bow up to your ear. Make strong... [fit] the arrow...' (figure 33).

The Sphinx Stela tells how the fully trained Amenhotep easily surpassed his father's record:

> He drew three hundred strong bows, comparing the workmanship of the men who had crafted them, so as to tell the skilled from the unskilled... Entering his northern garden, he found erected for him four targets of Asiatic copper, of one palm in thickness, with a distance of twenty cubits between one post and the next. Then his majesty appeared on the chariot like Monthu in his might. He drew his bow while holding four arrows together in his fist. Thus he rode northwards shooting at them... each arrow coming out at the back of its target while he attacked the next post. It was a deed never yet done; never yet reported.
>
> (Sphinx Stela of Amenhotep II. Lichtheim 1976: 41–2)

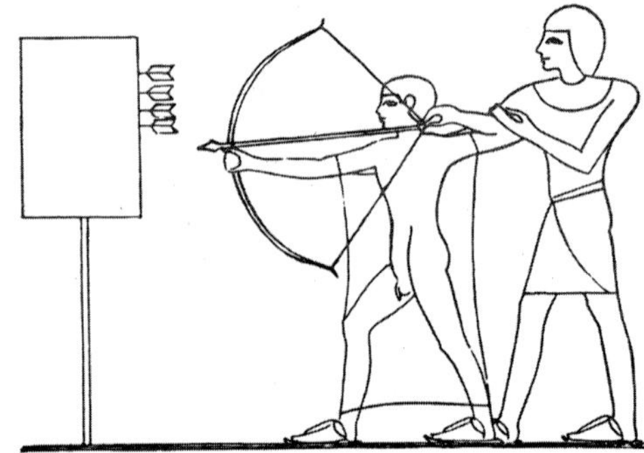

33. The young Amenhotep II learns archery from Min of Thinis. (After Touny and Wenig 1969, fig. 16)

34. The adult Amenhotep II shoots an arrow into a copper target from a moving chariot. (Block recovered from Karnak temple: housed in Luxor Museum)

35. Ay follows the precedent set by Amenhotep II. As a commoner Ay is known to have served as 'Overseer of the King's Horses' but he came to the throne as an old man, and this scene should not be read literally. Gold foil fragment recovered from KV58. (Cairo Museum JE57438)

The Karnak temple has yielded a granite block decorated with the image of Amenhotep II standing in his chariot to shoot at an ingot-shaped target (figure 34). Egypt's hunting/battle chariots served as mobile platforms for her archers and normally carried both a charioteer and a huntsman/soldier, but convention dictated that kings should be shown alone, driving with the chariot reins tied around their waist (figure 35).

So confident was Amenhotep II in his own physical abilities that he was prepared to throw caution to the wind and take part in a genuine contest. A now-broken stela raised at Medamud tells how Amenhotep first shot an arrow through a copper target three fingers deep, then offered a prize to anyone who could match his achievement. Unsurprisingly, no one could. When, in 1892, Victor Loret discovered Amenhotep II still lying in his sarcophagus in the Valley of the Kings (KV 35), he found the king's longbow, made from layers of horn, sinew and wood, lying by his side. This bow was stolen in 1900 and has never been recovered.

Big-game hunting

The New Kingdom expansion of the Egyptian empire allowed encounters with exotic big game (figure 36). Tuthmosis I reportedly

36. A New Kingdom king spears a lion. Limestone ostracon recovered from the Valley of the Kings. Howard Carter was convinced that the anonymous king is Tutankhamun. (Metropolitan Museum of Art 26.7.1453)

hunted elephants in Syria; his grandson, Tuthmosis III, definitely did. His feats were recorded in the autobiography of the courtier Amenemheb, who tells us with admiration that his king 'hunted 120 elephants for their teeth'. An inscription in the Armant temple tells how the same king 'brought down a rhinoceros with an arrow in the southern Nubian desert', while back home he claimed to have killed a herd of twelve wild bulls in just one hour.

Amenhotep III, not otherwise known as a sportsman, issued two sets of commemorative hunting scarabs, one to celebrate the slaughter of 102 (or 110) lions 'with his own arrows' during regnal years 1–10, and one to mark the killing of ninety-six wild bulls during regnal year 2. At Soleb, in Nubia, he built a large hunting park which served as a home for a variety of wildlife and which today survives as a series of post-holes. Two centuries later, Ramesses III provided the last illustration of a traditional chariot-riding huntsman-king by decorating his Medinet Habu mortuary temple with scenes of bull hunting.

Horses and races

Amenhotep II boasted of his affinity with horses, but whether he trained them to be ridden or to pull chariots is not made clear. While the imported eastern goddess Astarte regularly rides astride during the New Kingdom, the rare scenes of mortal riding feature army couriers rather than kings. There is no evidence for either formal horse races or formal chariot races, although the Sphinx Stelae raised by Amenhotep II and Tuthmosis IV both mention riding at speed. High-speed hunting brought its own dangers. Tutankhamun, who was buried with six complete but dismantled chariots and a wide range of composite bows, simple bows, arrows, slings, throwing sticks, boomerangs and clubs, may have met his untimely death in a hunting accident. The king's mummy shows extensive damage to the chest area that, if it was not caused in the embalming house, may well be the result of a high-speed impact.

Bull fighting and bull leaping

Wild bulls were accepted as symbols of male dominance and fertility, a symbolism made obvious by a scene on the prehistoric Narmer Palette that shows the king taking the form of a bull to gore an enemy. The first bull-hunting scene dates to the First Dynasty reign of Aha. From this time onwards there is ample evidence for bull hunting and for bull and cow cults, and there is a limited amount of evidence for other bull-based activities. Bull fighting (bulls fighting each other, rather than men fighting bulls) featured in several Upper and Middle Egyptian Old Kingdom tombs, with Akhmim cemetery providing the best representations.

The fortified Avaris palace of Ahmose, first king of the Eighteenth Dynasty, was decorated with frescoes depicting vibrant bull-leaping scenes set against a maze-like background which presumably represents the bull-leaping ground. These scenes are so similar to scenes found on the walls of the contemporary palace of Knossos that it seems that Ahmose must have employed a Minoan artist to depict the purely Minoan ritual of bull leaping.

Hunting in the marshes

Danger lurked in Egypt's waterways and swamps. Crocodiles were a constant menace, the bane of boatmen and laundrymen, linked with the disruptive god Seth, and feared and revered in equal measure. The classical authors, struck by this ambivalent attitude, tell us how, during the Graeco-Roman Period, the peoples of Thebes and the Faiyum revered the crocodile, the peoples of Dendera hated it, and the people of Elephantine dined off crocodile meat. Plutarch (*De Iside et Osiride* 50) tells us that the people of Edfu had an annual crocodile hunt. Aelian (*De Natura Animalitum* X 21, 24) tells us that at Dendera crocodiles were caught in nets, hung from trees, beaten to death and then eaten. Herodotus confirms that there were several methods of crocodile hunting but describes only one:

> They bait a hook with a chine of pork and let it float out into midstream. At the same time, standing on the bank, they take a live pig and beat it. The crocodile, hearing the squeals, makes a rush towards the live pig, finds the bait, gulps it down and is hauled out of the water. The first thing the huntsman does when he has landed the crocodile is to plaster its eyes with mud. This done, it is dispatched easily enough – otherwise it will give a lot of trouble.
>
> (Herodotus *Histories* II: 70)

Although crocodiles appear in river scenes from Predynastic times onwards, the first crocodile-spearing scene does not appear until the New Kingdom, when crocodile hunts are used to illustrate Chapter 31 of the *Book of the Dead*: 'Repulsing the crocodile which comes to carry away the magic spells'. Star charts featuring crocodile-spearing scenes were included in several New Kingdom tombs, including the tombs of Ramesses VI (KV 9) and Ramesses VII (KV 1). The temples of Edfu and Dendera have preserved images and associated texts describing Ptolemaic ritual crocodile slaughter.

Hippopotamus hunts

Under normal circumstances the hippopotamus, Egypt's largest

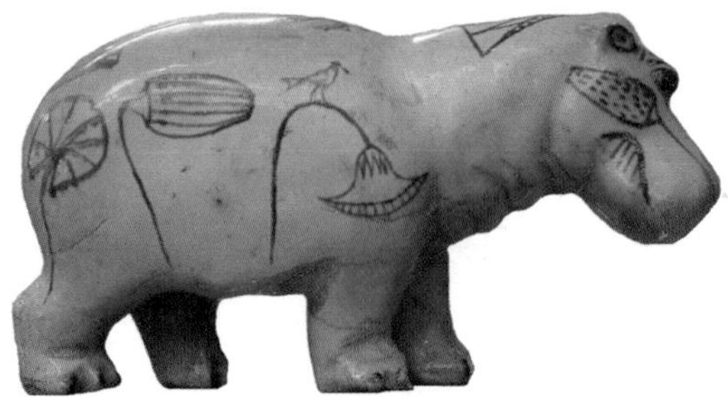

37. Middle Kingdom faience hippopotamus. (Cairo Museum)

indigenous animal, posed little threat to human safety, but the farmers whose crops could be devastated by a band of hungry hippopotami perceived them as a menace (figure 37). Once roused, the peaceful hippopotamus could become very dangerous – a worthy foe for a king.

One of the earliest hippopotamus hunts is featured on a seal belonging to the First Dynasty king Den and shows the valiant king standing upright in a fragile papyrus boat to harpoon his quarry. Clearly this is an exaggeration; it would take more than one harpoon thrust to kill a thick-skinned hippopotamus and, indeed, the next and quite impossible scene shows Den wrestling with the beast. Hippopotamus hunting as a royal sport seemed to lose its appeal after the onset of the Old Kingdom, although two statuettes recovered from Tutankhamun's tomb show the king poised to dispatch a hippopotamus single-handed. By this time hippopotamus hunting was no longer an exclusively royal pursuit, and the elite, too, are able to participate (figure 38).

Hippopotamus hunting features, somewhat obliquely, in the Twentieth Dynasty story *The Quarrel of Horus and Seth*, which tells how the two gods agree to determine who will rule Egypt by transforming into hippopotami and surviving underwater for three months. The competition comes to an abrupt halt when Isis, mother of Horus, decides to intervene to protect her son:

> She took a length of flax and twisted it into a rope. Next she fetched an ingot of copper, melted it, and cast it in the form of a harpoon. She tied the rope to the harpoon, and threw it into the water at the point where Horus and Seth had vanished beneath the waves. Under the water the harpoon bit into the flank of Horus, who gave a loud shriek. 'Help me mother, tell your barb to let me go, for I am your son, Horus.' Isis ordered her harpoon to release Horus, and threw it again into the water. This time it bit into the flesh of her brother, and it was Seth's turn to give a loud wail. 'What harm have I ever done to you, Isis? I am your brother, yet you hate me more than you would hate a complete stranger.' Hearing his words, Isis was greatly moved and once again she commanded her harpoon to release its victim.

In this version of the story Seth loses his throne but survives to sail for eternity in the solar boat of Re. But at Edfu, where the annual Ptolemaic Festival of Victory included a re-enactment of the drama, the contest ended with Seth, again in the form of a hippopotamus, mortally pierced by ten harpoons. His body was subsequently dismembered and eaten. Naturally the hippopotamus came to be identified with the disruptive Seth, and scenes of kings harpooning hippopotami can be interpreted as Horus (the living king) triumphing over chaos.

Fowling and fishing

An ill-preserved Eighteenth Dynasty text, *The Pleasures of Fishing and Fowling*, outlines for us the joy felt by Egypt's elite as they set off for the marshes, where they hope to 'trap birds by the thousands'. Fowling and fishing scenes decorate just one royal tomb (Ay: WV 23), but many private ones. They show hunters in delicate papyrus boats, poised to bring down marsh birds with curved throwing sticks or boomerangs. Throwing

38. Intef and his family hunt hippopotamus in the marshes. New Kingdom Theban tomb of Intef. (After Decker and Herb 1994, pl. 201)

39. Kheti harpoons a fish in his Beni Hasan tomb; one of a series of unfinished images showing boating, fishing and fowling in the marshes. (After Newberry 1893, pl. 11)

sticks are generally the preserve of men, although scenes of ritual dancing show both male and female dancers wielding curved throwing sticks.

In tomb scenes dating to the Fifth Dynasty and later, the elite hunters are often accompanied by their smaller-scale wives and children, who sit, inactive, in the papyrus boat. These charming scenes may be interpreted as images designed to promote rebirth, with the word for throwing stick, *kema*, also representing the verb 'to conceive'. Images of the stick-wielding elite may also be read as the commoner equivalent of the traditional royal smiting scene, which, as featured on the Narmer Palette, shows the king raising one arm to strike the foe (representative of chaos) who grovels at his feet.

Larger quantities of birds were caught using traps and nets, although it is doubtful whether or not this wholesale killing should be classed as a sport. Scenes of gods and kings netting birds and small game occasionally feature on temple walls, where they are generally interpreted as symbolic representations of the imposition of order over chaos. Commercial fishermen, too, used nets and traps, while sportsmen used spears or pronged harpoons to stab individual fish (figure 39). A decorated ivory chest recovered from his tomb shows a seated Tutankhamun using a bow and arrow to shoot both fish and birds, while his wife, Ankhesenamun, squats at his feet and hands him arrows.

Numerous bone and copper fish-hooks testify to the popularity of angling from Predynastic times onwards. The earliest anglers used a simple line and hook, and it was not until the Middle Kingdom that the rod developed. Angling remained a lower-class occupation – a necessary source of food, rather than a sport – throughout the Old and Middle Kingdoms and it is only in the Eighteenth and Nineteenth Dynasties that we find tomb owners and their wives fishing (figure 40). Invariably it is the tomb owner who holds the rod while his wife helps him by removing the caught fish from the hook.

40. Fishing with a rod in the Nineteenth Dynasty Theban tomb of Nebwenenef. (After Sahrhage 1998, pl. 37)

6
Martial arts

Wrestling

The Fifth Dynasty Saqqara tomb of the vizier Ptahhotep shows pairs of naked boys wrestling, one of the boys being Ptahhotep's own son. Six pairs appear on the tomb wall, but they should be interpreted as the same two boys demonstrating different moves in one continuous, cartoon-like fight.

By the Middle Kingdom wrestling had become a display sport, performed alongside dance and stick fighting in both religious and secular celebrations. Several three-dimensional wrestling models have survived (figure 41), and the Beni Hasan tombs include over two hundred images of wrestling pairs, the combatants painted different shades to allow the viewer to make sense of their movements (figure 42). Nine tombs include wrestling, with published scenes coming from the

41. (Above) Painted limestone model of Middle Kingdom wrestlers, from Abydos. (Ashmolean Museum)

42. Wrestling pairs in the tomb of Baqet III. (After Newberry 1893, pl. 5)

43. New Kingdom ostracon depicting men wrestling. (Cairo Museum)

tombs of Amenemhat (Tomb 2: 59 pairs), Baqet III (220 pairs), Kheti (122 pairs) and Baqet I (Tomb 29: 6 pairs). These tombs also include scenes of military life, and it is not clear whether the wrestlers are amateurs, professional entertainers or, as seems most likely, soldiers who have been taught to wrestle as part of their training. In the contemporary el-Bersheh tomb of Neheri there is a referee who stands between the opponents and orders them to 'do what you will'. As in the tomb of Ptahhotep, the majority of the Middle Kingdom wrestlers are naked, but some wear a short kilt, while others wear a broad belt apparently designed to allow their opponent to get a good grip.

The New Kingdom offers fewer tomb scenes of wrestling, but more sketches of wrestlers scribbled on ostraca (figure 43). By this time wrestling had become a part of royal ceremonial – a physical representation of the imposition of order over chaos – and the wrestlers had abandoned nudity in favour of a short kilt. A damaged block recovered from Amarna shows a pair of foreigners, almost certainly Nubians, grappling with each other, their kilts decorated with swinging spheres or weights. Wrestlers also appear in the Amarna tomb of Meryre II in scenes depicting the tribute celebration or *durbar* of Akhenaten's year 12. The Theban tomb of Tjanuni (TT 74) shows a group of Nubian wrestlers accompanied by a flag or standard, suggesting that they are an elite wrestling force.

Nubians, Libyans and Asiatics, the traditional enemies of Egypt, appear below the Window of Appearance in the Medinet Habu mortuary temple of Ramesses III, where, in front of a distinguished audience of Egyptian elite and foreign dignitaries, they are about to grapple with (and lose to) Egyptian wrestlers. The wall scene shows seven pairs of wrestlers, three pairs of stick fighters and a referee. At the end of each bout, with the foreigner suitably defeated, we see the victor standing over his fallen opponent, both arms raised in a gesture of triumph. Whether or not the bouts were fixed to ensure that the Egyptian always did win is not clear. The artists decorating the temple wall, of course, would never dream of depicting anything other than total Egyptian victory.

Although wrestling is represented many times and is occasionally accompanied by a brief caption such as 'I grab you on the leg!', 'I cause your heart to weep!' (both from Beni Hasan) or 'Watch out! I am seizing your leg and throwing you on your side in the presence of the king!' (Medinet Habu), it does not feature in the written records. This means that we are ignorant of the Egyptian name for the sport and know of no formal rules. It seems clear from the illustrations that wrestlers were allowed to seize any part of the opponent's body, and it is likely that the bout continued until one of the opponents was incapable of continuing. Few of the scenes show wrestlers on the ground.

Stick fighting

Sticks were a common feature of male Egyptian life. Nobles carried sticks to emphasise their authority, minor criminals were punished with floggings, schoolboys were beaten to encourage them to learn, and soldiers carried an arsenal of throwing sticks, fighting sticks, clubs and spears. During the New Kingdom some soldiers carried short metal swords and scimitar-like daggers too, but these weapons were both expensive and better suited to piercing and slashing than to duelling. Stick fighting or fencing, in contrast, is likely to have played an important role in army training (figure 44).

The first, indirect, reference to stick fighting comes from the Old Kingdom *Pyramid Texts*: Spell 324 mentions the fighting stick of Horus, while Spell 469 mentions the human stick fighters of Letopolis. By the New Kingdom stick fighting had become an accepted exhibition sport or ritual, and stick fighters (almost invariably soldiers) often perform alongside wrestlers. There are stick fighters on the broken Amarna wrestling scene already discussed, and stick fighters entertained Ramesses III and his guests alongside the wrestlers at Medinet Habu.

44. Stick fighters on the north pylon of the Ramesseum. (After Decker and Herb 1994, pl. 319)

Here we can see the fighters bowing to the crowds before their bout; later the victor stands before his king, arms raised, while his opponent hangs his head and hides his face in ritual shame.

The Eighteenth Dynasty tomb of Kheruef at Sheikh abd-el Gurna, Thebes (TT 192), shows stick fighters armed with soft papyrus stalks, performing exhibition matches in connection with the ceremony of raising the *djed* pillar during the celebration of the *heb sed* of Amenhotep III (figure 45). The presence of two referees and the brief captions

45. New Kingdom stick fighters using papyrus stalks for ritual combat in the Theban tomb of Kheruef. (After Decker 1992, pl. 58)

accompanying the scene, 'hit two times', suggest that a scoring system was in operation.

Stick fighting continued into the Ptolemaic Period, allowing the historian Herodotus (*Histories* II: 63) to witness, but not fully comprehend, a ritual fight at Papremis, at a time when Egypt was under Persian rule:

> As the sun draws towards setting, only a few of the priests continue to employ themselves about the image of the god, while the majority, armed with wooden clubs, take their stand at the entrance to the temple. Opposite there is another crowd of men, more than a thousand strong, also armed with clubs and consisting of men with vows to perform... A vigorous tussle ensues in which heads are broken and not a few actually die of the wounds they receive. That, at least, is what I believe, although the Egyptians told me nobody is ever killed.

Although some fighters wielded a stick in each hand, and the longer, heavier sticks must have been used double-handed, the majority fought with a single stick held in the right hand and a narrow protective shield or board fastened to the left forearm extending from elbow to fingers. Illustrations suggest that further protection was offered by padding covering the chin and forehead. Some of the earlier fighting sticks had curved ends, but by the New Kingdom most were straight, often with a woven hand-guard to aid the grip and protect the fingers. Some were weighted at the tip.

Kings are never shown fencing, yet Tutankhamun was buried with 130 assorted sticks and staves, including throwing sticks, walking sticks, ceremonial sticks and wide-ended fighting sticks.

Boxing

Boxing was a popular sport throughout the ancient Mediterranean world but, judging by the paucity of illustrations, was relatively rare in Egypt. Because of the essentially static nature of Egyptian art, the distinction between wrestlers and boxers, and even between dancers and boxers, is not always as obvious as we might wish. The tomb of Kheruef, however, shows kilted bare-knuckle boxers participating alongside other martial artists in the celebration of raising the *djed* pillar, while two figures in the Amarna tomb of Meryre may also be boxers.

7
Water sports

Swimming

Egyptian life – Upper Egyptian life in particular – was very much focused on the Nile. The river and its canals served as a source of water for people, animals and plants, and as a highway, laundry and sewer. Meanwhile, the secluded, shaded villas of the elite were furnished with handsome pools suitable for fishing and paddling. Given this emphasis on water, it seems likely that swimming was considered an important skill. Unfortunately it is a skill that is rarely recorded, although the autobiography in the First Intermediate Period tomb of Kheti II at Asyut confirms that elite children were taught to swim: 'He [the king] had me instructed in swimming along with the royal children.' The fictional *Quarrel of Horus and Seth*, already quoted in Chapter 5, features a form of underwater swimming competition, but there is no other evidence for competitive swimming or diving as a sport.

Realistic images of swimmers are rare; they include scenes of fishermen diving to release nets, girls swimming to catch birds, and hieroglyphic signs (figure 46), and a hapless battalion of Hittite soldiers swimming (and in some cases drowning) to escape the Egyptian troops features in Ramesses II's various illustrations of the battle of Kadesh. Less realistically, numerous New Kingdom cosmetic spoons take the form of a naked serving girl gliding through water, her outstretched arms supporting the bowl of the spoon, which occasionally takes the form of a duck or fish. These spoons are matched by bowls that show girls swimming to catch fish or ducks.

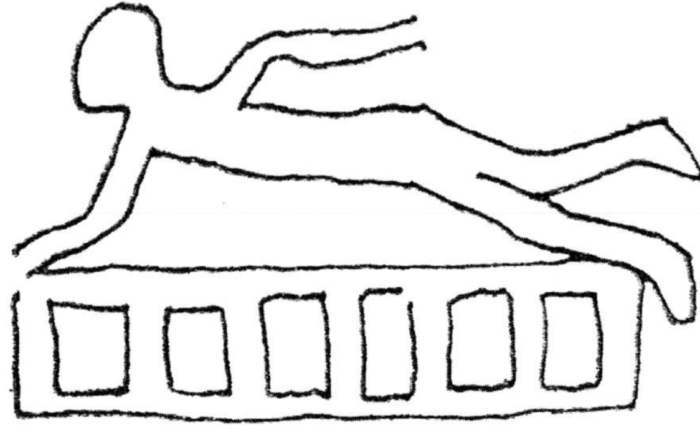

46. Swimming hieroglyphic determinative.

47. Hunting in the marshes was a male ritual. On the wall of their Giza tomb (G7530/7540) queens Meresankh III and Hetepheres II, her mother, take to the waters not to hunt or race but to perform the ritual of 'rustling the papyrus'.

Rowing and boat racing

The Quarrel of Horus and Seth tells how, after their aborted swimming competition, the two would-be kings competed to build and race stone boats. Horus, who did not trust Seth, built a wooden boat that he plastered and painted so that it looked like a ship carved from stone. Of course, when the race started, Seth's boat sank while Horus's boat floated. Far less strenuous is the rowing display described in the Middle Kingdom tale preserved on the Second Intermediate Period document today known as *Papyrus Westcar*, which tells how the jaded Old Kingdom monarch Sneferu watched entranced as boats full of maidens dressed in fishnet costumes rowed up and down the palace lake (figure 47).

There is little evidence for more formal boat races, although Amenhotep II boasts on his Sphinx Stela of his ability to steer a boat crewed by two hundred men over an impressive distance of three *iteru* (about 20 miles or 32 km). Tomb and temple images have allowed experts to reconstruct the distinctive New Kingdom rowing style, which seems to have been a

48. An Old Kingdom scene of fishermen jousting. (Cairo Museum)

mixture of standing (at the beginning of the stroke) and sitting (during the pull) action in a broadly circular movement.

Fishermen's jousting

Scenes of fishermen's jousting – crews of between four and six men in each papyrus boat apparently attempting to push their rivals into the water or strike them with their long punting poles – are known from the Old and Middle Kingdoms (figure 48). This sport was dangerous enough for those who could not swim but became doubly dangerous when the local crocodiles took an interest. Whether it was a regular, organised sport or simply a spontaneous outbreak of fun is not now apparent.

8
Acrobatics and dance

The Sixth Dynasty Saqqara tomb of Kagemni shows female athletes performing a gravity-defying display of high kicks. In the Middle Kingdom tombs of Beni Hasan female athletes dance, juggle and perform flips with a partner (tomb of Kheti, figure 49), while male athletes perform headstands (Kheti) and ballet-style pirouettes (Baqet III, figure 50) or cartwheel on and off a partner's back (Amenemhat). Eighteenth Dynasty carvings from Hatshepsut's Red Chapel at Karnak

49. Young girls perform acrobatic dances in the tomb of Kheti, Beni Hasan. (After Newberry 1893, pl. 13)

50. A male dancer, wearing a loincloth, performs a pirouette in the Beni Hasan tomb of Baqet III. (After Newberry 1893, pl. 7)

show a troop of processional dancers who include bridges, handsprings and cartwheels among their accomplishments. At all times there is a very thin line between dance and rhythmic acrobatics or gymnastics and, as the Egyptians saw no need to distinguish between the two, it would seem

51. A scantily dressed acrobatic dancer featured on a New Kingdom ostracon. (Turin Museum 7052; photograph: Angela Thomas)

pointless to try to separate them here.

Costume was adapted to allow the extravagant dance manoeuvres and, while throughout the dynastic age the majority of Egypt's women wore ankle-length garments, dancers routinely chose clothing that would allow them the required freedom of movement. Old Kingdom dancers regularly appear in short skirts with crossed straps over the chest. By the New Kingdom it is not uncommon for female acrobatic dancers to perform naked – but heavily made-up, and wearing elaborate jewellery – or with a simple belt slung around the hips (figure 51). Hairstyles, too, are adapted to the dance and, although many female dancers adopt short styles, others grow their hair long and weight it with bone or pottery disks (*ibau*) or heavy beads to create an eye-catching swing. Male dancers, who are in the minority, and who tend to appear in ritual rather than secular performances, wear short kilts and short hair.

Informal and secular dance

With no single generic Egyptian verb 'to dance', several words were used in association with particular dance styles or movements. These words are not explained in the literary sources – dance being apparently too well understood to need any explanation – but when matched to accompanying illustrations they can be partially understood. They include *iba* (the most commonly used non-specific term, often translated as 'jig' or 'caper'; the same word was used for the 'dancer' playing pieces on the *senet* board), *khebi* (acrobatic dancing), *rewi* (where the dancers carry clappers) and *tjeref* (a male dance of the Old Kingdom).

While ethnographic parallels suggest that dance was known and enjoyed

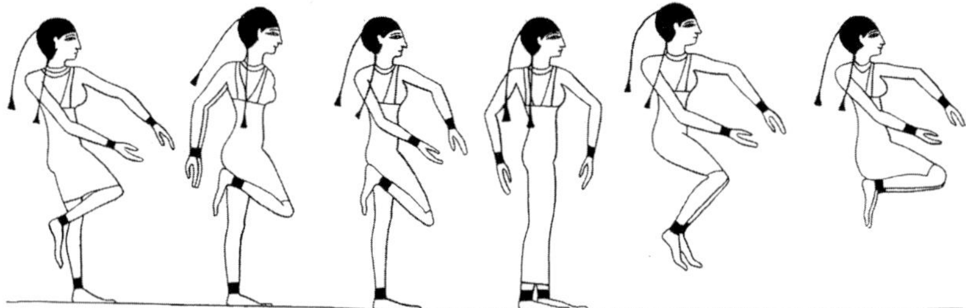

52. Jumping dancers in the tomb of Baqet III. (After Newberry 1893, pl. 4)

as far back as Palaeolithic times, there is little evidence for dance as simple recreational activity enjoyed by the masses (figure 52). Spontaneous, informal dance is assumed to have occurred at times of family and local celebration – at the welcoming home of a traveller, as briefly mentioned in the Middle Kingdom *Tale of Sinuhe*, for example – but, by their very nature, these ephemeral celebrations are rarely recorded and leave no archaeological evidence. References to men and women dancing together are particularly scarce, leading to the supposition that, as in modern traditional Egypt, men and women danced at the same time, but separately. The New Kingdom scribe Ani recommends celebrating the feast day of a patron god with 'song, dance and incense'; copious amounts of wine would allow the celebrants to communicate with Hathor, mistress of drunkenness and dance. Pointless dancing was, however, a bad thing, and time wasters were ridiculed as 'one who dances in the desert'.

In contrast, there is a great deal of evidence for professional or semi-professional dance as secular entertainment. In the absence of theatres, circuses and other places of mass entertainment this was largely a private luxury, although we cannot rule out the possibility that itinerant dancers performed outdoors. While larger estates may have employed their own permanent dance troupes, freelance dancers could be hired for a specific occasion; the Middle Kingdom tale recorded on *Papyrus Westcar* tells how four goddesses disguised themselves as travelling dancing girls.

The elaborate banqueting scenes found in New Kingdom tombs suggest that formal

53. Two young dancers entertain at a banquet in the New Kingdom tomb of Nebamun. The New Kingdom artists were better able to represent the fluid dance moves than their Middle Kingdom predecessors. (Photograph: Angela Thomas)

dance, accompanied by mainly percussive music, may have been standard entertainment in elite households (figure 53). These primarily secular images carry a secondary ritual message: not only do the lithe and lovely dancers entertain the living, they symbolise and stimulate the sexual potency of the deceased. Dancing scenes disappear from tomb walls at the end of the New Kingdom.

Ritual dancing

The earliest evidence for Egyptian dancing comes from Predynastic desert rock art and from Naqada I graves, which have yielded female clay figurines with narrow, bird-like faces and long arms raised above their heads, and painted pottery whose dancing female forms are often identified as goddesses. Already dance had developed strong religious connotations, and these would continue to the end of the dynastic age. Thus we find on the Scorpion Macehead, one of Egypt's oldest ritual objects, a row of at least four dancing women performing with one leg raised and hands poised to clap. The women are dressed in identical knee-length skirts and have long braided hair.

From the Old Kingdom onwards the elaborate elite funeral ritual included several forms of dance. The female 'ladies of the acacia house' performed their stately moves outside the embalmer's workshop after the completion of the mummification process. As the mummy processed to the tomb it was accompanied by the more acrobatic *iba* dancers, whose gyrations were perhaps intended to stimulate the deceased. From the late Old Kingdom onwards, male *muu* dancers donned short kilts and tall crowns constructed from woven marsh plants to perform a vigorous

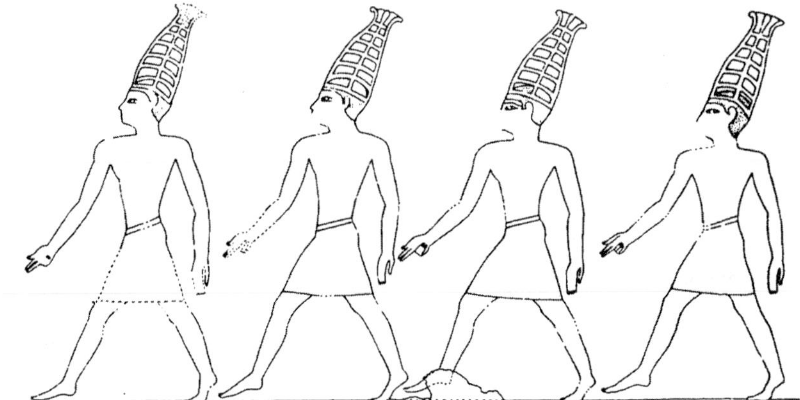

54. *Muu* dancers performing in the Middle Kingdom Theban tomb of Antefoker. (After Davies 1920, pl. 22)

high-stepping dance of welcome and guidance in the necropolis (figure 54).

Singers and musicians performed at religious festivals from the Old Kingdom onwards. The role of the temple dancers is less well recorded, although a Twelfth Dynasty papyrus recovered from the temple of Senwosret II at Lahun (Griffith 1898) provides some welcome detail, listing the names and nationalities of the temple dancers/acrobats and the dances they performed at a series of festivals including the New Year Festival, the Night Festival of Welcoming the Nile Flood and the Sand Removal Festival. The carved stone walls of the New Kingdom temples confirm that, while it is by no means certain that dance played any part in daily cult ritual, dance did play an important role in festival and processional ritual, including the Theban Festival of the Valley and Opet Festival, both festivals of renewal and regeneration. Dance was also an important aspect of rituals concerning the goddess Hathor. The queen and princesses who danced to welcome Sinuhe home rattled their sistra and *menyt* beads, and in so doing transformed their performance into a Hathoric ritual.

Dwarves and childbirth

Dancing dwarves, more accurately pygmies, were much prized as ritual dancers; they danced before their king just as the king might dance before the gods, they performed at high-status funerals and in temples, and they featured in the *Pyramid Texts*, where their dance formed part of the mortuary ritual. When the Sixth Dynasty child-king Pepi II wrote to praise the explorer Harkhuf for bringing him such a dwarf, Harkhuf recorded his king's letter on the right side of the entrance to his Aswan tomb:

> You state that you have obtained a pygmy, one of the god's dancers, from the land of the horizon-dwellers. And you add that this pygmy is like the pygmy that the God's Seal Bearer Wer-Djed-Ba brought from the land of Punt during the reign of King Isesi. But, as you point out, your pygmy is the first of his kind to come to Egypt from Yam. This is excellent news indeed. You really know how to please your Lord... Make your way northwards to the palace, at once. Hurry, and bring with you the remarkable pygmy from the land of horizon-dwellers, so that he might perform the dances of the god and delight my heart. Guard this pygmy with your life! When he is on board the ship, make sure that he is well supervised lest he fall into the water and drown. When he is in bed at night, have your loyal men care for him in his tent. Check on him at least ten times each and every night! For I long to see this remarkable pygmy more than I covet all the precious gifts of Punt.

55. The dwarf demi-god Bes on a block from the Graeco-Roman temple of Hathor at Dendera.

The connection between dance and birth – or rebirth after death – was particularly strong. For three millennia the lion-headed dwarf demi-god Bes danced and played music to frighten away the evil spirits who threatened women in labour (figure 55), while the early Old Kingdom 'ladies of the *khenert*' specialised in dances connected with childbirth and funerals. By the Fifth Dynasty these ladies had been joined by male colleagues, making the original translation of the word *khenert* as 'harem' obviously inappropriate. The link between dance and childbirth could be a very practical one; the four goddesses who, in *Papyrus Westcar,* disguised themselves as itinerant dancing girls were also expected to act as midwives.

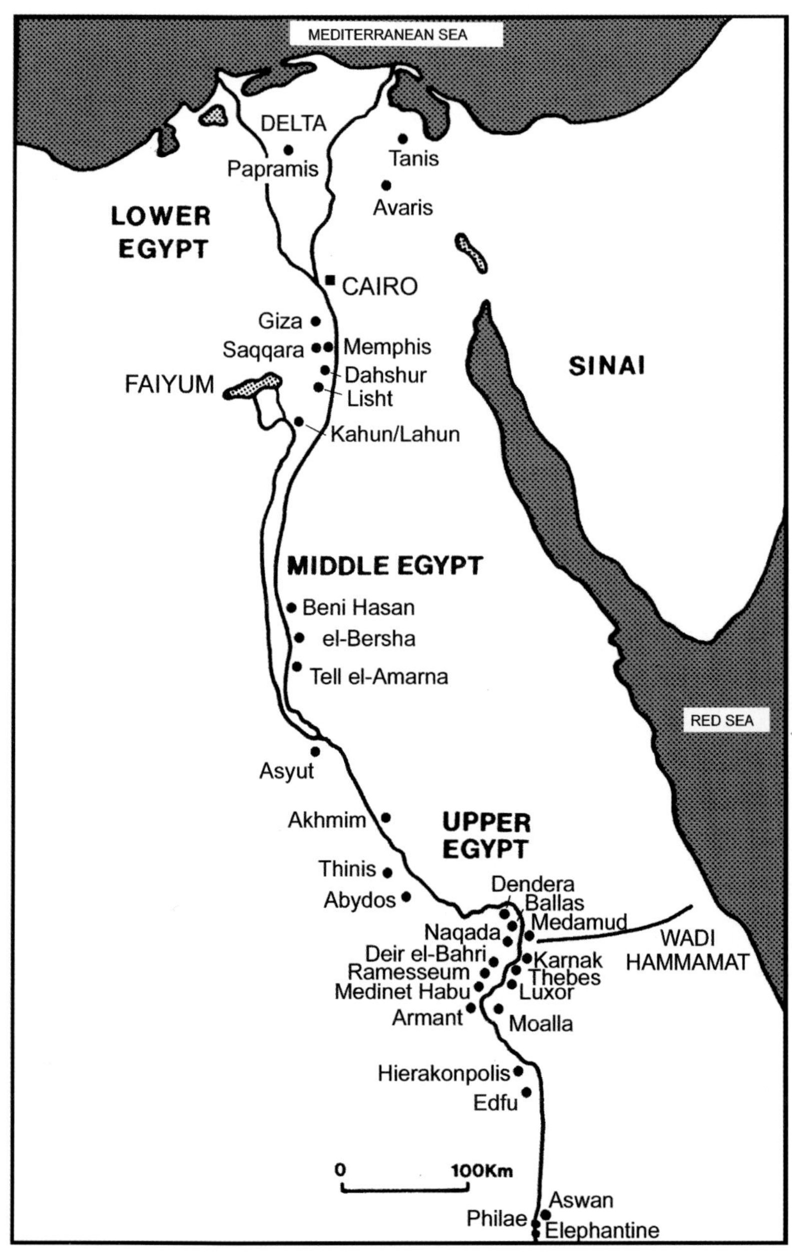

56. Map of Egypt showing the location of sites mentioned in the text.

9

Museums

The best collection of games, toys and sporting equipment is to be found in the Egyptian National Museum, Cairo. Few western museums have material in their collections directly relating to Egyptian sports, but several house individual game boards, game pieces and children's toys. It is advisable to enquire about specific items and about the opening times of any museum before arranging a visit. Many of the museums listed below have websites that display part or all of their collections. Readers might also be interested in consulting the website of the Griffith Institute, Oxford (www.ashmolean.museum/Griffith.html), which includes *Tutankhamun: Anatomy of an Excavation* – a complete database of Howard Carter's excavation.

Great Britain

Ashmolean Museum of Art and Archaeology, Beaumont Street, Oxford OX1 2PH. Telephone: 01865 278000. Website: www.ashmolean.org

The British Museum, Great Russell Street, London WC1B 3DG. Telephone: 020 7323 8000. Website: www.thebritishmuseum.ac.uk

The Manchester Museum, University of Manchester, Oxford Road, Manchester M13 9PL. Telephone: 0161 275 2634. Website: www.museum.man.ac.uk

The Petrie Museum of Egyptian Archaeology, University College London, Malet Place, London WC1E 6BT. Telephone: 020 7679 2884. Website: www.petrie.ucl.ac.uk

Royal Museum of Scotland, Chambers Street, Edinburgh EH1 1JF. Telephone: 0131 247 4422. Website: www.nms.ac.uk

Egypt

The Egyptian National Museum, Tahrir Square, Kasr-el Nil, Cairo 11557. Website: www.egyptianmuseum.gov.eg Displays the Tutankhamun treasures, including game boards and playing pieces and a wide range of archery equipment.

Luxor Museum of Egyptian Art, Sharia Nahr el-Nil, Luxor. Displays the Amenhotep II shooting scene.

France

Musée du Louvre, Palais du Louvre, 75058 Paris Cedex 1. Website: www.louvre.fr

Italy

Museo Egizio, Palazzo dell Accademia delle Scienze, Via Accademia delle Scienze, 10123 Torino (Turin). Website: www.museoegizio.org Displays dancing girl ostracon.

United States of America

Metropolitan Museum of Art, 1000 Fifth Avenue at 82nd Street, New York, New York 10028. Website: www.metmuseum.org Displays lion-spearing ostracon.

10
Further reading

Translations of dynastic and classical texts

Caminos, R. A. *Literary Fragments in the Hieratic Script*. Griffith Institute, Oxford, 1956.

De Sélincourt, A. (translator). *Herodotus: The Histories*. Penguin, London, 1954. Revised with introduction and notes by J. M. Marincola, 1996.

Faulkner, R. O. *The Ancient Egyptian Pyramid Texts*. Clarendon Press, Oxford, 1969.

Lichtheim, M. *Ancient Egyptian Literature: A Book of Readings II: The New Kingdom*. University of California Press, Berkeley, 1976.

Oldfather, C. H. (translator). *Diodorus Siculus 1: Books I–II*, 1–34. Heinemann, London, and Harvard University Press, Cambridge, Massachusetts, 1933.

Tyldesley, J. A. *Tales from Ancient Egypt*. Rutherford Press, Bolton, 2004.

Games and toys

Borghouts, J. F. 'The evil eye of Apophis', *Journal of Egyptian Archaeology*, 59 (1973), 114–150.

Carnarvon, Earl of, and Carter, H. *Five Years' Exploration at Thebes: A Record of Work Done 1907–1911*. Oxford University Press, London, 1912.

David, A. R. 'Toys and games from Kahun in the Manchester Museum collection', in J. Ruffle *et al* (editors), *Glimpses of Ancient Egypt*. Aris & Phillips Ltd, Warminster, 1979, 12–25.

Kendall, T. 'Games', in D. B. Redford (editor), *The Oxford Encyclopedia of Ancient Egypt*. Oxford University Press, Oxford, 2001, 2: 1–3.

Petrie, W. M. F. *Kahun, Gurob and Harawa*. Kegan Paul, London, 1890.

Piccione, P. *Gaming with the Gods: The Game of Senet and Ancient Egyptian Religious Beliefs*. Abstract published on www.cofc.edu/~piccione/senet_web.html 2003; book forthcoming, Brill, Leiden.

Piccione, P. 'Mehen, mysteries and resurrection from the coiled serpent', *Journal of the American Research Center in Egypt,* 27 (1990), 43–52.

Pusch, E. B. *Das Senet-Brettspiel im Alten Ägypten*. Münchner Ägyptologische Studien 38, Munich and Berlin, 1979.

Quibell, J. *Excavations at Saqqara (1911–12): The Tomb of Hesy*. Institut Français, Cairo, 1913.

Tait, W. J. *Game Boxes and Accessories from the Tomb of Tutankhamun*. Griffith Institute, Oxford, 1982.

Sport and dance

The books and articles listed below represent the more accessible sources, with preference given to those in English. A more extensive bibliography may be found in Wolfgang Decker's *Annotierte Bibliographie zum Sport im alten Ägypten* (Verlag, St Augustin, 1978).

Altenmüller, H. 'Hunting', in D. B. Redford (editor), *The Oxford Encyclopedia of Ancient Egypt*. Oxford University Press, Oxford, 2001, 2: 130–133.

Brunner-Traut, E. *Der Tanz im Alten Ägypten nach bildlichen und inschriftlichen Zeugnissen*. Glückstadt, Hamburg and New York, 1938.

Davies, N. de G. *The Tomb of Antefoker, Vizier of Sesostris I and of His Wife Senet (No 60)*. Egypt Exploration Society, London, 1920.

Davies, N. de G. *The Mastaba of Ptahhetep and Akhethetep at Saqqareh, 1*. Egypt Exploration Society, London, 1900.

Decker, W. *Sport and Games of Ancient Egypt* (translated by A. Guttmann). Yale University Press, New Haven, 1992.

Decker, W., and Herb, M. *Bildatlas zum Sport im Alten Ägypten*. Brill, Leiden, New York and Cologne, 1994.

De Vries, C. E. 'A ritual ball game?', in *Studies in Honour of John A. Wilson*. Oriental Institute of the University of Chicago, Chicago, 1969; 25–35.

Gillam, R. *Performance and Drama in Ancient Egypt*. Duckworth, London, 2005.

Griffith, F. Ll. *Hieratic Papyri from Kahun and Gurob*. Quaritch, London, 1898.

Jarrett-Bell, C. D. 'Rowing in the VIIIth Dynasty', *Ancient Egypt* (1930), 11–19.

Lexová, I. *Ancient Egyptian Dances* (translated by K. Haltmar). Oriental Institute, Prague, 1935; revised with introduction by D. Bergman, Dover, New York, 2000.

Newberry, P. E. *Beni Hasan II*. Kegan Paul, London, 1893.

Piccione, P. 'Sportive fencing as a ritual for destroying the enemies of Horus', in E. Teeter and J. A. Larson (editors), *Gold of Praise: Studies on Ancient Egypt in Honour of Edward F. Wente*. Oriental Institute of the University of Chicago, Chicago, 1999, 335–49.

Reeder, G. 'The mysterious Muu and the dance they do', KMT 6:3, Fall (1995), www.egyptology.com/reeder/muu

Sahrhage, D. *Fischfang und Fischkult im alten Ägypten*. Philipp von Zabern, Mainz am Rhein, 1998.

Säve-Söderbergh, T. *On Egyptian Representations of Hippopotamus Hunting as a Religious Motive*. Horae Soderblomianae, Uppsala, 1953.

Shedid, A. G. *Die Felsgräber von Beni Hassan in Mittelägypten*. Zaberns Bildbände zur Archäologie 16, Mainz, 1994.

Simpson, W. K. *The Mastabas of Qar and Idu, G7101 and 7102*. Giza Mastabas 2, Boston Museum of Fine Arts, Boston, 1976.

Spencer, P. 'Dance in ancient Egypt', *Near Eastern Archaeology,* 66:3 (2003), 111–121.

Touny, A. D., and Wenig, S. *Sport in Ancient Egypt* (translated by Joan Becker). Edition Leipzig, Leipzig, 1969.

Vandier, J. *Manuel d'Archéologie Égyptienne IV, Bas-Reliefs et Peintures. Scènes de la Vie Quotidienne.* Picard, Paris, 1964.

Wilson, P. 'Slaughtering the crocodile at Edfu and Dendera', in S. Quirke (editor), *The Temple in Ancient Egypt: New Discoveries and Recent Research*. British Museum Press, London, 1997: 179–203.

Index